This book is a gift to a
very special person

Benjamin

from: _Sunday School_

For
Shanda
&
Riley

My Jesus Pocketbook of the
LORD'S PRAYER
This book was created by **STIRRUP ASSOCIATES, INC.**

written and illustrated by
GINGER ADAIR FULTON

edited by **Bonnie Harvey** and **Cheryl Phillips**

in consultation with
Rev. Mark Gutzke, Ph.D.
and
Ray Harvey
in its production

I am Tobin, and this is my big sister Gingerbread. She helps me get ready for bed.

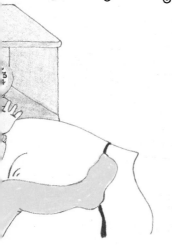

Gingerbread tells me, "It's time to say your prayers, so get your Bible."

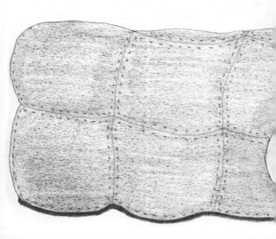

"In the Bible, Jesus tells us a special way to pray. It's called 'The Lord's Prayer.'"

Then Gingerbread began to
read "The Lord's Prayer"
to me:
"Our Father which art
in heaven, Hallowed be
Thy name..."
And so I prayed:
You are my Father
who lives in heaven;
Your name is very
holy and special.

Again Gingerbread read:
"Thy kingdom come..."
Then I prayed:
I'm waiting and
watching until the
time You come to
take me to Your
house to live.

Once more, Gingerbread read:
"Thy will be done in
earth, as it is in
heaven..."
So I prayed:
I want the whole
world to follow Your
plans -- as the angels
in heaven do right
now.

Next, Gingerbread read:
"Give us this day our
daily bread."

And so I prayed:
Today give me the
food I need to help
me grow strong
and tall.

Then, Gingerbread read:
  "And forgive us our
  debts, as we forgive
  our debtors."
I prayed:
  I'm sorry I don't
  act like You want
  me to all the time.
  Please forgive me.

I'm going to
forgive everyone
who does bad
things to me, too.

The next part of the prayer Gingerbread read went like this:

"And lead us not into temptation..."

So I said to God:

Take my hand and lead me only to the places You want me to go.

And Gingerbread read:
"But deliver us
from evil..."
Then I prayed:

When I want to
do bad things,
help me run away
fast!

Then, Gingerbread read:

"For Thine is the
kingdom, and the
power, and the
glory, for ever.
Amen."

So I told God:

You are more
wonderful than
I can begin to think
about, and You are
very, very strong.
All things everywhere
belong to You, and
always will.

Amen.

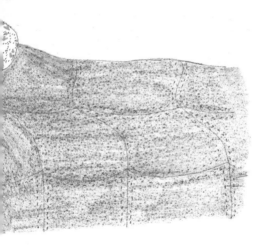

Our Father which art in heaven, Hallowed be thy name. Thy kingdom come. Thy will be done in earth, as it is in heaven. Give us this day our daily bread. And forgive us our debts, as we forgive our

debtors. And lead us not
into temptation, but
deliver us from evil: for
thine is the kingdom,
and the power, and the
glory, for ever. Amen.

Matthew 6:9-13

Other publications available featuring

Gingerbread & Tobin

My Jesus Pocketbook of
God's Fruit

Other "My Jesus Pocketbooks"
available:

My Jesus Pocketbook of Nursery Rhymes
My Jesus Pocketbook of ABC's
My Jesus Pocketbook of Scripture Pictures
My Jesus Pocketbook of The 23rd Psalm
My Jesus Pocketbook of Li'l Critters
My Jesus Pocketbook of Manners

Please contact your local
Christian bookstore or write:

David C. Cook Publishing Co.
Elgin, IL 60120